Oxford Read and Discover

1 Discover!

At the Beach

Rachel Bladon

OXFORD
UNIVERSITY PRESS

OXFORD
UNIVERSITY PRESS

Great Clarendon Street, Oxford, OX2 6DP, United Kingdom

Oxford University Press is a department of the University of Oxford. It furthers the University's objective of excellence in research, scholarship, and education by publishing worldwide. Oxford is a registered trade mark of Oxford University Press in the UK and in certain other countries

ISBN: 978 0 19 464628 4

An Audio Pack containing this book and an Audio download is also available, ISBN 978 0 19 401235 7

This book is also available as an e-Book, ISBN 978 0 19 410836 2.

An accompanying Activity Book is also available, ISBN 978 0 19 464649 9

Printed in China

This book is printed on paper from certified and well-managed sources.

ACKNOWLEDGEMENTS

Cover photograph: Shutterstock (Shell on beach/ EpicStockMedia)

Illustrations by: Kelly Kennedy pp 6, 9, 15; Alan Rowe pp 20, 21, 22, 23, 24, 25, 26, 27, 28, 29, 30, 31.

The Publishers would also like to thank the following for their kind permission to reproduce photographs and other copyright material: Alamy pp 4 (high tide/low tide/Maximillian Weinzierl), 6 (agefotostock), 7 (whale/Stephen Frink Collection), 8 (rockpool/Design Pics, Inc), 15 (pelican/Chris Gomersall), 17 (sand dunes/Sean Pavone), 19 (Juergen Schwarz); Getty Images pp 11 (Paul Kay/Photodisc), 12 (Ozflash/iStock), 13 (dolphin/ Stuart Westmoreland/Image Source), 15 (oystercatcher/ Roger Tidman/Corbis Documentary), 18 (kitesurfer/David Pu'u/The Image Bank); Naturepl.com p 7 (periwinkle/Robert Thompson), 8 (crab/Tui De Roy), 10 (Jane Burton), (13 (shark/ Dan Burton), 14 (Kim Taylor); Oxford University Press pp 3 (Corbis), 5 (Photolibrary), 16 (Shutterstock), 17 (stack and arch/ Shutterstock), 18 (snorkelling/Shutterstock); Science Photo Library p 9 (starfish/Fred Winner/Jacana); Shutterstock p 7 (barnacles/Tartmany).

 # Introduction

At the beach, the ocean meets the land. Many amazing plants and animals live there.

What can you see at the beach? What animals live there?

 Now read and discover more about the beach!

The Beach

Every day the ocean goes up the beach at high tide, and it goes down the beach at low tide.

High Tide

Low Tide

The ocean moves with the wind, too. The wind makes waves. The ocean is salt water. It's big and strong.

The ocean can break rocks and shells into pieces. The pieces of rock and shell hit the water and other rocks. Then they get very little. This is how the ocean makes rocks and shells into sand.

waves

sand

shell

Go to page 20 for activities.

2 Sand and Rocks

What can you see in the sand and on the rocks at the beach?

At low tide the tellin shell hides under the sand. It hides there because other animals like to eat it. It gets food and water with one of its siphons.

A Tellin Shell

siphon

A Flat Periwinkle

The green flat periwinkle hides in green seaweed. Can you see it here?

Barnacles

The barnacle lives on rocks. Its shell grows onto the rocks, so it doesn't move when there are waves.

Discover!

Some barnacles grow on whales!

barnacles

Go to page 21 for activities.

3 In Rockpools

A Rockpool

At low tide, the ocean moves down the beach. Then you can find rockpools.

A Crab

claw

Let's look in a rockpool. Here's a crab. It gets food with its big, strong claws. It eats barnacles, starfish, and other little animals. It eats plants, too.

clam

Discover! The starfish can put its stomach out of its mouth! Then it can eat this big clam.

Crabs eat starfish, and starfish eat clams. This is called a food chain.

crab

A Food Chain

starfish

clam

→ Go to page 22 for activities.

 # Near the Beach

Many fish and other little animals live in the water near the beach. There's lots of food for them there.

The prawn eats seaweed and little animals.

Discover! The prawn has 20 legs. It walks with 10 legs, and it swims with 10 legs!

The seahorse eats very little fish.
It eats very, very little animals
and plants called plankton, too.

A Seahorse

See how this seahorse hides in the
seaweed. In this green seaweed,
the seahorse is green, but in yellow
seaweed, it's yellow!

→ Go to page 23 for activities.

5 In the Ocean

A Seal

You can see some amazing animals in the ocean.

Here's a seal. The seal lives in the ocean and on land. When it swims in the ocean, it puts its head out of the water to get air.

blowhole

A Dolphin

The dolphin jumps out of the water, and little fish are scared. They swim away, and then the dolphin can catch them! The dolphin gets air with a blowhole on its head.

On sunny days, the basking shark swims at the top of the ocean. It can eat lots of plankton there. Plankton is its favorite food.

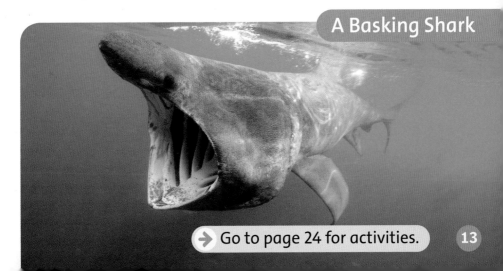

A Basking Shark

Go to page 24 for activities.

6 In the Air

Puffins

Many birds live near the beach. There's lots of food for them there.

The puffin lives on cliffs. When it's hungry, it flies down and swims under the ocean. Then it catches its favorite fish!

The pelican can catch lots of fish in its big bill. It opens its bill and the water goes out. Then it can eat the fish.

bill

A Pelican

A pelican can get 11 liters of water in its bill!

Oystercatchers don't eat oysters! They eat mussels. They open the shells with their bill.

An Oystercatcher

mussel

Go to page 25 for activities.

7 At the Coast

At the coast near the beach, there are cliffs. Some waves hit hills on the coast, and pieces of land break into the ocean. This makes cliffs.

Sometimes there are holes in the cliffs. The ocean hits the holes and makes caves.

Cliffs

cave

stack

arch

The ocean can make arches and stacks, too.

At the coast, the sand moves in the wind. Then the sand makes hills called sand dunes.

Discover!

Sand dunes can move 100 meters in a year.

➜ Go to page 26 for activities.

8 Fun at the Beach

A Kitesurfer

You can do many things at the beach! You can kitesurf, and the wind moves you on the ocean. You can snorkel, too. Then you can see amazing fish in the water.

A Snorkeller

flag

The ocean is big and strong. Don't go away from the people you know. Look for flags – they tell you where and when you can swim.

Have fun at the beach, but remember the ocean plants and animals. Keep the beach clean for plants, animals, and other people.

→ Go to page 27 for activities.

① The Beach

← Read pages 4–5.

1 Match.

1 The ocean

2 At low tide

3 Sand

4 At high tide

is little pieces of rock and shell.

is salt water.

the ocean goes up the beach.

the ocean goes down the beach.

**2 Complete the puzzle.
Then find the secret word.**

1 → r o c k s

2 →

3 →

4 →

5 →

The secret word is:

2 Sand and Rocks

← Read pages 6–7.

1 Match. Then write the numbers.

1 The tellin shell   lives on rocks.

2 The flat periwinkle   hides under the sand.

3 The barnacle   hides in seaweed.

☐   ☐   1

2 Order the words.

1 with / gets / food / The / a siphon. / tellin shell

The tellin shell gets food with a siphon.

2 barnacle's / rocks. / onto / grows / The / shell

_____

3 grow / Some / whales. / on / barnacles

_____

← Read pages 8–9.

1 Write the words.

crab   starfish
~~rockpool~~   clam

1 _rockpool_
2 _____
3 _____
4 _____

2 Complete the sentences.

clams   ~~rockpools~~   barnacles
stomach   claws

1 You can find _rockpools_ at low tide.

2 The crab gets food with its _____ .

3 The crab eats _____ , other little animals, and plants.

4 The starfish can put its _____ out of its mouth.

5 Crabs eat starfish, and starfish eat _____ .

4 Near the Beach

← Read pages 10–11.

1 Draw and write.

1  This is a prawn. The prawn walks with 10 legs, and it swims with 10 legs!

2  This is a seahorse.

2 Circle the correct words.

1 Near the beach, there's lots of **(food)** / **legs** for little animals.

2 Plankton are very, very **big** / **little** animals and plants.

3 The prawn has **ten** / **twenty** legs.

4 The prawn walks and **flies** / **swims** with its legs.

5 In green seaweed, the seahorse is **green** / **yellow**.

⑤ In the Ocean

← Read pages 12–13.

1 Write the words.

> basking shark   seal   dolphin

1 _____   2 _____   3 _____

2 Circle the correct words.

1 The seal puts its head out of the water to get **food** / **air**.

2 The dolphin gets air with a blowhole on its **head** / **nose**.

3 The dolphin can catch little **fish** / **birds**.

4 The basking shark's favorite food is **crab** / **plankton**.

6 In the Air

← Read pages 14–15.

1 Write the words. Then write the numbers.

puffin   pelican   oystercatcher

1 It has a big bill.

_____

2 It lives on cliffs.

_____

3 It eats mussels.

_____

2 Write *true* or *false*.

1 There's no food for birds at the beach.   *false*

2 The puffin can swim, but it can't fly.   _____

3 The pelican catches fish in its big bill.   _____

4 The pelican can get 13 liters of water
   in its bill.   _____

5 Oystercatchers eat oysters.   _____

6 Oystercatchers eat mussels.   _____

7 At the Coast

← Read pages 16–17.

1 Write the words.

cliffs   ocean   stack
sand dunes   arch   cave

1 _____   3 _____   5 _____

2 _____   4 _____   6 _____

2 Complete the sentences.

sand dunes   coast   caves   cliffs

1 You can see cliffs, caves, stacks, and arches at the _____ .

2 Pieces of land break into the ocean, and this makes _____ .

3 Hills of sand are called _____ .

4 Holes in cliffs are called _____ .

8 Fun at the Beach

← Read pages 18–19.

1 Find and write the words.

a	s	u	n	e	o	w
p	e	o	p	l	e	t
s	p	l	a	n	t	s
h	d	o	l	p	h	s
e	d	f	l	a	g	o
a	n	i	m	a	l	s

1 _people_   2 f _____

3 a _____   4 p _____

2 Answer the questions.

At the beach, do you ...	Yes, I do.	No, I don't.
snorkel?		
kitesurf?		
swim?		
play in the sand?		
look in rockpools?		

Project

At the Beach

1 Draw and write about what you can see at the beach.

1

This is ___a prawn.___
What I know about it:
___It eats seaweed___
___and little animals.___

2

This is _____
What I know about it:
_____
_____

3

This is _____
What I know about it:
_____
_____

4

This is _____
What I know about it:
_____
_____

2 Complete the food chain.

clam starfish crab

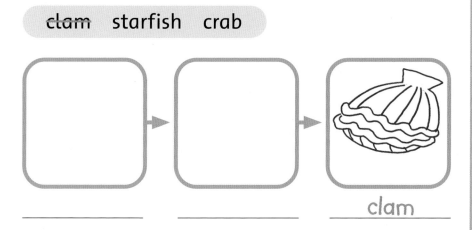

_____   _____   clam

3 Make more food chains.

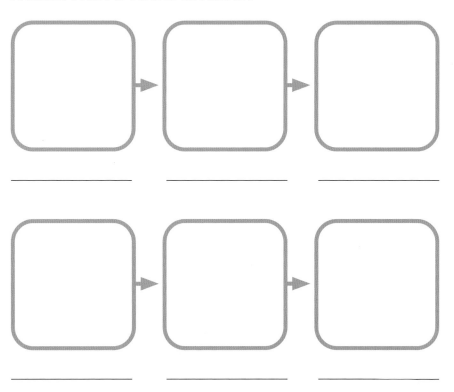

Picture Dictionary

air

animals

beach

break

clean

cliffs

coast

down

food

grow

hide

hill

hole

land

near

ocean

oyster

people

pieces

plankton

plants

rocks

salt

sand

sand dunes

seaweed

shell

stomach

strong

top

up

waves

Oxford Read and Discover

Series Editor: Hazel Geatches • CLIL Adviser: John Clegg

Oxford Read and Discover graded readers are at six levels, for students from age 6 and older. They cover many topics within three subject areas, and support English across the curriculum, or Content and Language Integrated Learning (CLIL).

Available for each reader:
- Audio Pack
- Activity Book

Available for selected readers:
- e-Books

Teaching notes & CLIL guidance: **www.oup.com/elt/teacher/readanddiscover**

Subject Area / Level	The World of Science & Technology	The Natural World	The World of Arts & Social Studies
1 — 300 headwords	• Eyes • Fruit • Trees • Wheels	• At the Beach • In the Sky • Wild Cats • Young Animals	• Art • Schools
2 — 450 headwords	• Electricity • Plastic • Sunny and Rainy • Your Body	• Camouflage • Earth • Farms • In the Mountains	• Cities • Jobs
3 — 600 headwords	• How We Make Products • Sound and Music • Super Structures • Your Five Senses	• Amazing Minibeasts • Animals in the Air • Life in Rainforests • Wonderful Water	• Festivals Around the World • Free Time Around the World
4 — 750 headwords	• All About Plants • How to Stay Healthy • Machines Then and Now • Why We Recycle	• All About Desert Life • All About Ocean Life • Animals at Night • Incredible Earth	• Animals in Art • Wonders of the Past
5 — 900 headwords	• Materials to Products • Medicine Then and Now • Transportation Then and Now • Wild Weather	• All About Islands • Animal Life Cycles • Exploring Our World • Great Migrations	• Homes Around the World • Our World in Art
6 — 1,050 headwords	• Cells and Microbes • Clothes Then and Now • Incredible Energy • Your Amazing Body	• All About Space • Caring for Our Planet • Earth Then and Now • Wonderful Ecosystems	• Food Around the World • Helping Around the World